Illusions

by

Ivan Viripaev

in a translation by Cazimir Liske

Illusions was commissioned by and premiered
at the Theater Chemnitz on 29 September 2011
directed by Dieter Boyer.

Actors Touring Company premiered the English translation
of Illusions at Wickham Theatre, University of Bristol
on 24 April 2012.

CAST

Derbhle Crotty *First Woman*
Cazimir Liske *Second Man*
Rona Morison *Second Woman*
Jack Tarlton *First Man*

CREATIVE TEAM

Ramin Gray *Direction*
Lizzie Clachan *Design*
Charles Balfour *Lighting*
Alex Caplen *Sound*
Jim Arnold *Casting*

PRODUCTION TEAM

Steve Wald *Production Manager*
Altan Reyman *Company Stage Manager*
Charlotte Jobson *Technical Stage Manager*
Natasha Piper *Design Assistant*

THANKS

Brigitte Auer, Paul Handley, Mark Hornsby, Richard Lee
and all at the Jerwood Space, Joanna Marston, Lucy Maycock
and all at North Wall, Laurence Mitchell, Richard Rudnicki,
Rachel Shipp, Stephanie Walsh, Graham Whybrow
and all our rehearsal room Mystery Guests.

The Actors Touring Company's licence to present
Ivan Viripaev's play *Illusions* is granted by Rosica Colin Limited,
London, in conjunction with Henschel Schauspielverlag, Berlin.

BIOGRAPHIES

Derbhle Crotty   First Woman

For Actors Touring Company: *Crave*.

Theatre credits include: *The Beauty Queen of Leenane* (Young Vic), *Macbeth*, *Macbett*, *The Penelopiad*, *Hamlet*, *Little Eyolf*, *Camino Real*, *I'll be the Devil* (RSC), *The Merchant of Venice*, *Summerfolk*, *Playboy of the Western World* (NT), *The Weir*, *Alice Trilogy* (Royal Court), *The Home Place* (Comedy and Gate, Dublin), *Royal Supreme* (Drum, Plymouth) *The Playboy of the Western World*, *The Good Father*, *Sive*, *The Silver Tassie*, *The Gigli Concert* (Druid Theatre), *Marble*, *An Ideal Husband*, *The Three Sisters*, *Dandy Dolls*, *Portia Coughlan*, *The Mai*, *The Well of the Saints*, *A Month in the Country* (The Abbey Theatre Dublin), *Dancing at Lughnasa* (Gate) T*he Field* (Olympia Theatre), *The Winter's Tale* (Corcadorca).

TV includes: *The Clinic, Any Time Now*.

Film include: *Stella Days, Notes on a Scandal, Inside I'm Dancing, Poorhouse*.

Jack Tarlton   First Man

For Actors Touring Company: *Crave, The Golden Dragon, Making the Sound of Loneliness.*

Other theatre includes: *Beasts and Beauties* (Hampstead Theatre & Bristol Old Vic), What Every Woman Knows (*Finborough*), *The Merchant of Venice, A Midsummer Night's Dream, Twelfth Night, The Taming of the Shrew* (Propellor, UK & International tours), *The Deep Blue Sea* (Theatre Royal Bath, Vaudeville & UK tour), *The Sexual Neuroses of Our Parents* (Gate), *She Stoops to Conquer* (Manchester Royal Exchange), *Coram Boy, Once in a Lifetime* (NT), *The Man Who* (Orange Tree), *Romeo and Juliet* (Chichester), *Afore Night Come* (Young Vic), *An Inspector Calls* (Garrick), *Troilus and Cressida, A Month in the Country* (RSC).

TV includes: *Doctors, The Golden Hour, Dead Ringers, Doctor Who, The Genius of Mozart, Swivel on the Tip, Hearts and Bones, Life Support, Wings of Angels*, T*he Cater Street Hangman*.

Film includes: *The Unscarred*

Cazimir Liske   Second Man / Translator

Born in Denver, USA, Caz trained at the Moscow Art Theatre School.

For Actors Touring Company: *Crave*.

Other theatre includes: *Illusions* (Praktika), *Lafkadio* (Masterskaya), *Woe from Wit* (Moscow Art Theatre), *Riverside Drive* (Meyerhold Centre), all in Moscow. Also *Stravinsky.Games* (Baryshnikov Arts Centre, NY), *Comedy of Errors* (Moore Theater, New Hampshire).

Film and TV includes: *Interns, Law and Order, Plain Girl, Wedding Swap, Shadow-Boxer 2, The Diaries of Dr Zaitsevsa.*

Translations: *Illusions, The Delhi Dance, If This Is a Man*

Rona Morison   Second Woman

For Actors Touring Company: *Crave*.

Rona trained at Guildhall School of Music and Drama where credits include *Dear Brutus*, *The House of Atreus*, *DNA* and *Badenheim 1939*.

Film includes: *Love Bite*. This is Rona's professional stage debut.

CREATIVES

Ivan Viripaev

Ivan Viripaev is a Russian playwright, director and screenplay writer. He was born on August 3, 1974 in Irkutsk. Viripaev graduated from the Irkutsk Drama School in 1995 and worked as an actor and director in Irkutsk. He also founded the theatre group Play Space. In 1998, he graduated from the Moscow Drama School and worked from 2001 as a theatre director mainly at Theater.doc in Moscow. Since 2006 he has directed several of his own plays at Praktika Theatre in Moscow and written and directed his own movies. He also directed his own plays *July and Delhi Dance* which won awards at several Polish festivals. In 2011 Viripaev and his wife Karolina Gruszka were named People of the Year in Poland.

Theatre: *DreamWorks* (2011), *Illusions* (2011), *Comedy* (2010), *Delhi Dance* (2009), *July* (2006), *Genesis No 2* (2004), *Oxygen* (2003), *Valentine's Day* (2001), *The City Where I Am* (2001), *Dreams* (1999). Movies (written and directed by himself): *Euphoria* (2006), *Sensation* (2009, project Short-circuit), *Oxygen* (2009), *13 Texts Written in Autumn*.

Theatre awards include several in Russia, among others the Golden Mask Award for *Oxygen* and the International New Drama Festival Award for *Genesis* and *July*; the International 'Contact' Theatre Festival Award, Poland, for *Oxygen* and the Bansemer & Nyssen Playwright Award, Germany 2009.

Winner of several movie awards for *Euphoria* including the Leoncino d'Oro (Independent Youth Jury Award) at the 63rd Venice Film Festival (2006), Grand Prix at the 22nd International Film Festival in Warsaw, a Jury Special Award at Russian Film Festival Kinotavra 2006 and several movie awards for *Oxygen* at Kinotavra 2009 including best director, best music, and the White Elephant Critics' Prize.

Ramin Gray   Director

For Actors Touring Company: The Golden Dragon.

Other theatre includes: *Motortown*, *The Ugly One*, *The Stone*, *Terrorism*, *Over There*, *Ladybird*, *Way to Heaven*, *Woman and Scarecrow*, *Push Up*, *Just a Bloke* (all Royal Court),*The American Pilot*, *I'll be the Devil* (RSC), *Harper Reagan* (Salzburg Festspiele and Deutsche Schauspielhaus, Hamburg), *Orphans* (Schauspielhaus, Wien), *The Ugly One* (Praktika, Moscow), *Cat and Mouse* (Sheep) (Theatre National de l'Odeon, Paris), *The Child* (Gate), *A Message for the Broken-Hearted* (Liverpool Playhouse).

Opera includes: *Death in Venice* (Staatsoper Hamburg and Theater an der Wien), *Bliss* (Staatsoper Hamburg).

Ramin is currently Artistic Director of the Actors Touring Company.

Lizzie Clachan Designer

A co-founder of SHUNT and designer for all their productions. Theatre includes: *Jumpy, Wastwater, Our Private Life, Aunt Dan and Lemon, The Girlfriend Experience, On Insomnia and Midnight, Woman and Scarecrow* and *Ladybird* (Royal Court), *A Woman Killed with Kindness* (NT), *The Trial of Ubu, Tiger Country* (Hampstead), *I'll be the Devil, Days of Significance* and *The American Pilot* (RSC), *Happy Days* (Sheffield Crucible), *Bliss* (Staatsoper Hamburg), *Far Away* (Bristol Old Vic), *Gobbo and Julie* (National Theatre Scotland).

Charles Balfour Lighting Designer

Theatre includes: *Marilyn* (Citizens Glasgow), *Who's Afraid of Virginia Woolf* (Sheffield Crucible, Northern Stage), *Beauty Queen of Leenane* (Young Vic), *Now or Later, The Girlfriend Experience, The Ugly One* (Royal Court), *I'll be the Devil* (RSC), *Loot* (Tricycle), *Christmas Carol* (Kingston Swan) *The Weir* (Octagon Bolton), *Angels in America, The English Game* (Headlong), T*he Duchess of Malfi, Hedda Gabler, Don Quixote* (West Yorkshire Playhouse), *A Doll's House, Christmas Carol, Son of Man* (Northern Stage), *The Flint Street Nativity, The Tempest* (Liverpool Playhouse), *Cleansed* (Oxford Stage Company), *Hair, Woyzcek, Witness* (The Gate, Notting Hill), *Amadeus, Masterclass* (Derby Playhouse), *Baby Doll, Therese Raquin, Bash* (Citizens Glasgow), *Through the Leaves* (Southwark Playhouse, Duchess West End).

Alex Caplen Sound Designer

Alex is Deputy Head of Sound at the Royal Court.

Theatre (sound design) includes: *Ogres* (Tristan Bates); *Wanderlust* (Royal Court); *It's About Time* (Nabokov) *The Love for Three Oranges, Tosca* (Grange Park Opera); *Mine, Ten Tiny Toes, War and Peace* (Shared Experience); *Over There* (Royal Court & Schaubühne Berlin); *Stephen and the Sexy Partridge* (Old Red Lion/ Trafalgar Studios) *Peter Pan, Holes, Duck Variations* (UK Tour); *The Wizard of Oz, The Entertainer* (Nuffield Theatre); *Imogen* (Oval House/ Tour).

Theatre (operator/engineer) includes: *Wig Out!, Rhinoceros, The Arsonists, Free Outgoing, Now or Later, Gone Too Far, The Pain & The Itch* (Royal Court); Edinburgh Military Tattoo 2009 & 2010; *Bronte, Kindertransport* (Shared Experience); *Blood Brothers* (International tour); *Ballroom* (UK tour). Other work includes: large-scale music touring as Front of House mix engineer.

Jim Arnold Casting Director

Theatre credits include: *DNA* (Hull Truck); *Yerma* (Gate Theatre); *Pericles* (Regent's Park); *Matilda, The Musical* (RSC); *Lingua Franca* (Finborough & 59E59, New York); *Hortensia and the Museum of Dreams* (Finborough); *Fragile!, Le Mariage* (Arcola); *Artist Descending a Staircase* (Old Red Lion).

Film credits include: *Six Ways to Kill Your Lover* (Short Film).

ABOUT ACTORS TOURING COMPANY

Actors Touring Company presents the best in international contemporary theatre, on tour in the UK and internationally. The company produces the most innovative scripts from abroad, often commissioning its own translations and creating work collaboratively with artists from the UK and overseas.

We reach audiences through our national and international touring programme; through our digital engagement initiative which opens up the rehearsal and production process to anyone interested; and through The Salon, our developing programme of wrap-around events designed to stimulate debate, showcase artistic talent, present opportunity for emerging artists and provide outlets for the creativity of young people.

Staff

Ramin Gray   Artistic Director
Nick Williams   Executive Director
Charelle Griffith   Administrator
Jo Cottrell   Development & Marketing Associate
Edward Armitage   Finance Manager
Christine Twite   Collaborative Doctoral Student

Board of Directors

Maria Delgado   Chair
Nelson Fernandez   Vice-Chair
Ben Assefa-Folivi
Caroline Bailey
Chris Barnes
Caroline Firstbrook
Michael Quine
Hetty Shand

Actors Touring Company is a registered charity No. 279458, and is currently one of the National Portfolio of arts organisations funded by Arts Council England.

ACTORS TOURING COMPANY
NEEDS YOUR SUPPORT

Actors Touring Company asks you to consider supporting its work. In order to find and translate the very best international scripts, commission writers and translators, identify innovative talent and forge thrilling international creative collaborations, we need your help. In return we would be pleased to warmly welcome you in to the very heart of the Company's activities.

We hope you will consider supporting our work.

There are four levels of involvement.

Backstage Crew   £100 per annum
Actors' Angels   £500 per annum
Internationalists' Circle   £1,000 per annum
World Premier Circle   £5,000 or more per annum

Gift Aid it!

If you are a UK Income or Capital Gains taxpayer Actors Touring Company can reclaim 25p of tax on every £1 that you give. Higher rate taxpayers can claim the difference between basic and higher rate tax in their tax return, or gift it to charity.

For more information on the benefits of supporting the work of Actors Touring Company please contact **Jo Cottrell** on **020 7930 6014** or **jo@atctheatre.com.**

Our current supporters

Lisa Baker, Geraldine Brodie, Jo Cottrell, Prof M Delgado, Conor Fenton, Nelson Fernandez, Caroline Firstbrook, Genesis Foundation, David Lubin, Derek Richards, Ali Tomkinson, Saibh Young

DIRECTOR'S NOTE

Ivan Viripaev is a man of the theatre, an actor, director and writer from Irkutsk in Siberia who has made Moscow his home and where he has created an astonishingly consistent and highly original body of work over the last decade. His texts, and it is often appropriate to refer to them as texts as opposed to plays, seem to offer an enormous openness of interpretation and possibility for theatre makers but are in fact characterised by a steely determination to pursue their idiosyncratic journeys. There is often, as in *Illusions*, a clear gap between the performer (again, perhaps that is a better word than actor) and the text, by which I mean the issue of embodiment or incarnation often raises its head: who are these performers through whom reams of narrative flow effortlessly towards the spectator and why are they telling us the things they do? What exactly is their relationship to the tales they tell? It's clear they can't ever *be* the people they talk about in the sense one might find in a more conventional play.

These conundrums seem all the more tangible in *Illusions*, a text prefaced with a quote from Corneille's seminal *L'Illusion comique* of 1636. Corneille is explicit in his use of theatrical devices to take characters on journeys of discovery while constantly manipulating and distorting the perspective of the audience. This is what Viripaev excels at here, where the myths of love are held up, interrogated and often cruelly dismantled before the eyes of audiences of varying levels of credulity. But then what is love other than a complex series of stories we tell ourselves and the other? And also how high are the stakes in that game when it is played, as here, with deadly seriousness?

Viripaev engages his spectators by pulling them into the action of the drama: just like the characters we meet, we have to concentrate hard on the stories we're told, we have to weigh carefully the value of everything, we have to sharpen our antennae, otherwise we will be as lost in this theatre as the characters become in their lives. Our powerful human desire for narrative, for resolution, for clarity is here given a jolt as Viripaev leads us into a hall of mirrors where we sense we might be losing our grip and where we are forced to redefine our relationship to the existential issues of loyalty and betrayal, love and death, truth and fiction.

RAMIN GRAY
London, March 2012

Ivan Viripaev
Illusions

translated by Cazimir Liske

faber and faber

First published in 2012
by Faber and Faber Limited
74–77 Great Russell Street, London WC1B 3DA

Typeset by Country Setting, Kingsdown, Kent CT14 8ES
Printed in England by by CPI Group (UK) Ltd, Croydon CR0 4YY

A CIP record for this book
is available from the British Library

ISBN 978-0-571-29532-6

FSC
www.fsc.org

MIX
Paper from
responsible sources
FSC® C101712

2 4 6 8 10 9 7 5 3 1

Characters

First Woman
thirty

Second Woman
thirty

First Man
thirty-five

Second Man
thirty-five

ILLUSIONS

Toutefois, si votre âme était assez hardie,
Sous une illusion vous pourriez voir sa vie,
Et tous ses accidents devant vous exprimés
Par des spectres pareils à des corps animés.

Pierre Corneille, *L'Illusion comique*

*A Woman appears onstage. Then shortly after her a
Second Woman. Then a Man appears, then shortly after
him a Second Man. They have come only to tell the
audience a story about two married couples.*

First Woman Hello. I want to tell you about a married
couple. These were wonderful human beings. They lived
together for fifty-two years. Fifty-two years! Always
together. Their life was complete. A fulfilling life!
Extraordinarily beautiful love. Her name was Sandra, his
was Denny. When Denny turned eighty-two he became
very ill, lay down in bed and didn't get up. And one day
he sensed that right now he was about to die. He called
to his wife Sandra. She sat down next to the bed. Denny
took her by the hand and started speaking to her. He
managed to tell her everything he wanted to say.
Everything he needed to say.

He said:

— Sandra, I want to thank you. I want to thank you.

Pause.

— I am thankful to you for the life I have lived. Thanks
to you, I've lived a wonderful, amazing, fulfilling life. All
of this is thanks to you.

Sandra wanted to answer, but Denny asked her to be
silent. It was important for him to say all this. Sandra
understood that Denny was dying, she sat next to him
and didn't say a word. She looked at him, looked to see
him for the last time. To remember him as he was, alive.

7

Pause.

— I am thankful to you for teaching me about love. Because of you, I found out what love is, what the power of love is. That love is not a word, not romance, but work. Love is work, it is accepting responsibility. Sandra, thanks to you, I know what it is to be responsible. That's the most important thing there is – to be responsible for something. And to be thankful. To be thankful and to be responsible – there's the whole formula for life. Responsibility and thankfulness. Thank you, Sandra, thank you for your love. Your love taught me that life is devoting every instant of attention to someone dear. Loving you, I learned how to be attentive. I learned how to see others. Love teaches how to see others, and not only oneself. I loved you and understood that I must live up to that love, I must live up to you, to your love, and I changed. I was compelled to change. That is such a blessing, such a miracle – when someone makes you change! When you make a conscious effort and you change yourself. You came into this world as one being and you leave it as another. That means you really lived, truly lived. And the only thing that can teach us to live that way is love. Nothing is capable of recovering us from the abyss of egocentricity except love. Love forced me to hold up my head and look at myself objectively, love forced me to conquer my laziness, my cowardice, my fear. Everything I have gained in this life, I did all of it thanks to you, Sandra. I found I was loved by a woman like you and I wanted to be the man who was worth your love, and I undertook certain deeds for the sake of your love. And everything I have managed to do for other people, for the world, all of this I did fuelled by the energy of my love for you. And this love itself, at some point, became greater than just love for a woman, it suddenly went beyond its own boundaries and flung itself upon the whole world. Loving you I learned how to love others.

8

Sandra, the love you have given to me all these years –
fifty-two years, Sandra! – This love gave meaning not
only to my life, but to the lives of those around us. Our
children, our friends. I saw how my friends looked at us
and how they wanted to be like us, how they wanted to
love like us. And many of them changed their lives for
that reason. Your love, Sandra, it's like a powerful light,
it illuminates everything around it. Everything that
touches your love becomes something else, it changes,
transforms, blossoms. Thank you, Sandra, for your
integrity, for never compromising. Thank you for the
harsh words you sometimes addressed me with, thank
you for the unpleasant things you said to my face, thank
you for your rigidity. Sometimes I was offended listening
to you, sometimes I didn't like what I heard, but I am
especially thankful precisely for this. I was so angry at
times, so hurt by your words, but you told me the truth,
and that is precisely what saved me from the depths of
greed and self-love to which people are so often driven.
You were honest, you spoke from your heart, and thanks
to that fact I was able to avoid countless misfortunes.
Sandra, all our lives you have saved me from trouble.
You were my true guide and teacher. I am so thankful to
you for the life you have given me. For our beautiful
children, raised by you. It is thanks to you they are such
sensitive, kind people. And most of all, Sandra, most
of all, I want to thank you for telling me about love,
for teaching me how to love. For explaining to me what
love is. At our very first meeting you said to me –
remember? – you said that true love can only be mutual
love. That true love is when two people love each other,
and if only one person loves, there's no love to begin
with. I remembered these words my whole life. And in
every second of my life I remembered that love is two, and
that means I am responsible for your love. This empowered
me to escape many temptations. It empowered me to

never cheat on you with other women. Of course it's no secret that men look at other women, and I am no exception. But when I was on the verge of cheating on you I suddenly remembered your words, that love is mutual, love is reciprocity, and then I understood that my actions would betray not only my love, but yours as well. I made a conscious effort and avoided being unfaithful. I am so happy that we have lived these fifty-two years together and never once been unfaithful, and that we have nothing to hide from each other. And that I am dying in such a lovely way, such a beautiful death. Thank you for letting me die this way. It is such a joy, at the end of life, to be able to pronounce the words I've pronounced. This is what is meant by a fulfilling life, a life in love, in creation, and a dignified exit from this world. Thank you, my dearest, for all of this, for all of my life and my beautiful death. Forgive me for dying first, and leaving you with no one to tell everything I've told you. Of course it's selfish of me, Sandra, to die first, but alas there's nothing I can do – nature is stronger than our desires. I would like to be with you in the moment of your death, to sit like this close to you and look at you. I'm sure this is very hard, I know that dying is easier than living through the death of a loved one. I'm sorry that you should go through this with me of all people. But when you die, Sandra, remember these words of mine before your own death, and know that I will doubtless be somewhere nearby. My love will be with you. I don't believe in life after death. I know that today my journey ends and that there is no continuation beyond. But I believe and I know, Sandra, that love does not die, it lives on eternally, even after we've gone, our love will go on living. I can't explain this from a scientific point of view but I feel this is true. I don't believe in mysticism, I'm speaking about a simple, very simple thing. Love is a very simple thing reached by only a few. I lived through life to find that love exists. Love is a great power. Love conquers death. I am unafraid of dying. I love you.

And he dies.

Pause.

And Sandra sits close by and looks at her husband.

And now he's gone.

And she stands and leaves the room.

Pause.

And after the death of her husband, Sandra lived only one more year, and then became ill, lay down in bed and also felt one day that she was about to die. So then she asked her husband's friend to come visit her. His name was Albert. Albert and Denny were best friends, they had been friends since schooldays. They were inseparable all their lives. Albert was best man at Denny and Sandra's wedding. And when Albert entered the room, Sandra sensed more strongly than she had felt that whole previous year that Denny was gone.

She said:

— Sit down Albert, I want to tell you a few words before I die today – and I'm going to die today, I know this. And thank goodness it's so.

Albert wanted to answer, but Sandra asked him to be silent. It was very important for her to say all this.

— We've known each other, Albert, for over fifty years already, isn't that right? You are my husband's friend. You were the best man at our wedding. And, you know, I want to tell you that the very day when I first saw you was the day I met Denny. I came to meet Denny, and there you were. And you see, from that very minute and to this very day, all these years, these fifty-three years and four months, all this time I have loved only you, Albert. As soon as I saw you then, next to Denny, I knew right away that here was the man I was going to love forever. But you were married, and I saw that you loved your wife. And so I married Denny, and lived with him all these years, and you were always close by, and always, every second of my life I loved you and love you now and only here, as I die, I wish to tell you about this. But that's not all, Albert.

Pause.

I want to thank you for the joy that I've experienced, having been granted this rare opportunity to love. Thanks to my love for you, I learned what it means to wish for nothing for yourself, but only to give. My love for you taught me that giving is much more important than demanding something for yourself. I learned that loving is giving, that true love makes no demands, holds no claims. All these years, these fifty-some odd years I watched you and my heart was filled with this light and beautiful feeling. Of course I suffered from not being able to be close to you. I always wanted to be with you, I wanted intimacy, I thought about this, I thought about it almost constantly. But in thinking about you I was in fact with you, I was with my love for you. And this love, my love for you was felt by other people, my love for you was felt by everyone around me. My husband Denny felt this love. I never deceived him because within me was love, and part of this love I gave to him. I gave him part of my love for you. I was very honest with him, because I loved – not him, it's true – but within me was love and he took that love and was happy. When I was young I suffered terribly because I was sure that true love could only be mutual love, but then I realised that love has no rules or formulas. I realised that love is just love, it exists however and with whomever it wants. Love is this force that exceeds all boundaries and destroys all barriers. I loved you with no hope for requital, and from this my love became even stronger. And I became stronger. And I grew fearless. I grew bold. I was bold. Loving without hoping for requital taught me to be responsible for my feelings, taught me to look after my heart. I learned that love is something difficult to obtain, but very easy to lose. And I began to look after my love. Thank you for never letting me get close to you; you never looked at me as a woman, but always as the wife of your best friend. I don't know that I'd be able to hold myself back if I were given a chance to be close to you. But I truly respect and adore your lovely wife Margaret. She is an extraordinary, exquisite woman and you love her and that is beautiful. And I am happy that the man I love more than life itself is capable of love. I know that you are capable of love, and that is so beautiful. I wish you and Margaret happiness. I hope you will go on living together. Thank you, for meeting me on my life's journey, for being here, for existing. For the possibility of living in love. For the opportunity to learn that love is when you only give and demand nothing in return. Thank you for coming, for hearing me out, for letting me leave this life in such a beautiful and perfect way. I am happy to have a death like this. I was lucky that Denny died first, that I could see him off. He died very beautifully. And now I also die with a feeling I've lived for a purpose. I am unafraid of dying. I lived through life to learn that love exists. Love is a great power. Love conquers death. I love you.

And then she said:

— You don't have to say anything, Albert. I ask that you not answer me now. Now, just go. Goodbye. We won't see each other again. Say hello to Margaret. Be happy. Goodbye.

That's it. A little story.

Pause.

Second Woman Now I want to tell you about a second married couple. They also lived together for over fifty years. His name was Albert, hers was Margaret. They were both about eighty years old, they were precisely the same age. And one day Albert came home from a walk somewhere, sat in a chair in the middle of the room, called to his wife and asked her to come and sit before him in the wicker armchair. He said:

— I want to talk to you, Margaret. About something important. You and I haven't talked about what's important for a long time, have we?

— You and I, as far as I know, have never talked about what's important, answered Margaret.

She was a woman with a very fine sense of humour.

— That sure is funny, said Albert.

Then he went on.

— Margaret, I want to tell you that it turns out I've fallen in love with another woman. It's difficult for me to say this to you, but we've lived fifty-four years together and I've never intentionally deceived you. I respect you very much, you are the mother of my children . . .

— And the grandmother of your grandchildren, Margaret chimed in.

She was a woman with a fine sense of humour.

— Yes, yes, that's quite funny, responded Albert and then continued:

— So. I must tell you the very unpleasant truth. Margaret, for the first time in my life, I've learned what love is. What true love is, the love described in literature, the love that everyone dreams about when they're young and that nobody finds, and then everyone settles with whatever's on hand. We don't find true love and we decide that it doesn't exist, that it's all literary fantasy, and then we marry whoever's close by, whoever's real, whoever's convenient, and then we live with him or with her our whole lives, thinking that this is what humankind is capable of, that this is all the love there can be, but in fact love is something else entirely. Love isn't like this – this isn't love. Love is something completely different. Love exists, Margaret. It's just you and I weren't destined to experience it together, and we've lived together fifty-four years thinking that what we feel for each other is love, but that wasn't it – what we felt wasn't love. Love is entirely different, it has a different smell, different vibrations, different taste, a different colour, I came to realise this just today, Margaret. I came to know this only at the end of life, but I'm happy that at least now, even at the end of my life, it's finally happened to me. I am happy, but I'm also terribly sorry for you, Margaret. I don't want to seem ungrateful, you gave me the best years of my life – I mean, let's be honest, you gave me my whole life, and I'm immeasurably thankful to you. I cherish that fact, you are the closest person to me, you always have been and always will be, but I never loved you, Margaret, and you never loved me – I only just realised this, too, and, believe me, we never loved each other with the love that everyone dreams about in youth and that almost never actually happens with anybody – but you see, it happened to me. I'm happy, Margaret! I have loved, for the first time in my life. But I love another woman. I'm sorry.

And having said all this, Albert fell silent.

And here, of course, a short pause fell over the conversation. Not too long. And then Margaret said:

— Albert, you old fart. At first she said just that.

First Man Because she was a woman with a fine sense of humour.

Second Woman Yes, she was a woman with a fine sense of humour.

First Man And this, despite the fact that she had cancer. When she turned sixty, Margaret was diagnosed with breast cancer, she underwent surgery, had one breast removed, and she . . . Just joking. She didn't have cancer, and her breast was just fine. In fact, she was almost never sick at all with anything. She was a very healthy woman with a fine sense of humour.

Second Woman And so, when Albert had delivered his monologue on love, Margaret listened and as she listened her thoughts ran something like this: 'Jesus, he's just an old fart, why should I say anything, who knows what he's talking about? He just wants to make me angry, that's all. Why should I pretend to react to all his nonsense about love? We're both practically dead already, why should we go on discussing all this and getting our knickers in a twist, it's a bit too late for that already. I'd better just keep quiet and not give this old fool any occasion to fancy himself a young lover.' That's what she thought. But in truth for some reason Albert's big elaborate speech on love somehow had an effect on Margaret. And although she was an intelligent woman with a fine sense of humour, nonetheless at this particular moment intelligence and humour failed her, and though she had decided she wasn't going to answer this old fool, immediately after thinking that she wouldn't answer, she went along and answered.

She said:

— I only want to tell you, Albert, that you shouldn't make judgements about others based on yourself. If in the course of your life you weren't destined to know what love is, excuse me, but that in no way means that life worked out the same way for others.

— By 'others' you mean to say 'you'? said Albert.

— Yes, I mean to say me, answered Margaret.

— You mean you want to say that you happened to experience true love, is that what you're saying?

— Yes, that's precisely what I'm saying.

Here, Albert went up to Margaret, knelt down before her, covered his face with his hands, sat in this pose for a few minutes, and then uncovered his face, looked at Margaret and said:

— I'm very sorry, Margaret. But alas, you only think that you love me. Or rather, of course, you love me, just as I love you, but Margaret, I'm sorry, but I'm talking about an entirely different love, that you and I never felt.

— Well, there you go again speaking on behalf of others, Albert. You didn't feel it, others might have felt it.

— No, Margaret, 'others' – that is, you – never felt it, because true love can only be mutual love, and I literally found this out just today. Love can only be mutual love, requited love, and if one person loves another, but the other doesn't love the first, then it isn't love, and the love the first person feels isn't true love – he just thinks he loves. I found out about this literally just today, through my own experience. I didn't want to tell you the details, but since we've gotten in so deep already, I'll tell you. And again, forgive me for bringing you such pain.

— Forgiven, said Margaret. She was a woman with a fine sense of humour.

— That's funny, said Albert and continued:

— Today I was at Sandra's. She feels very sick and it seems she's dying. And so there I was at Sandra's and she told me that it turns out her whole life, all these years, she loved me. You see? Not Denny, but me! And it's true, why would she lie just before death? I could tell just from the way she said it that she wasn't lying. Her whole life she loved me and only me, but she couldn't confess her feelings to me, she couldn't betray Denny, couldn't wreck his life. And she said that earlier, she thought that true love could only be mutual love, requited love, but then, loving me, she realised that wasn't true, after all, her love for me was unrequited. And just as she was telling me this, I sat there listening to her, and my whole life connected with Sandra and Denny flashed before my eyes. I remembered Sandra when she was young, I remembered how we visited them every Saturday, remembered all our holidays together, our trips to the sea. I remembered Sandra, what a gorgeous woman she was, her gait, her lovely hands, hips, her personality, her modesty, her intelligence. I recalled how one day she burst into tears when Denny fried a snail on the grill along with the vegetables – remember? That was on your birthday! And for some reason I just remembered all of this. And listening to Sandra today I remembered that I had always liked her, liked her, but nothing more. And all of a sudden that thought struck me – 'liked her, but nothing more'. And I suddenly realised that here I was, standing before this old woman stretched out in bed, here I stood, and all of a sudden I realised I love her – you understand? Furthermore I suddenly realised that I'd always loved her, only that love had always been somewhere deep down, so deep that it was impossible for me to make out. Do you understand? This is very hard for me to explain. I didn't acquire this love just now, this love, it turns out, has always been with me. I just couldn't see it, I couldn't let it manifest, my mind was always engaged in something else.

You see, Margaret, nothing new has happened here. I've just suddenly learned that I always loved Sandra, and that it was true love, because it was mutual love, and we were made for each other – only for some reason I was unaware of all this, I was in some kind of strange unawareness. I don't know why it's happened this way, probably it was just a matter of time. The ripe fruit falls by itself. A cruel game of fate, or coincidence, I don't know. But the most important thing I want to tell you is that love didn't come to me today, it was with me always – but it awoke in me only today. And you see, Sandra was mistaken when she said her love was unrequited love. She simply didn't know, as I didn't know, that I love her. Her love was requited love, because I always loved her. True love cannot be unrequited love. Therefore, I'm so sorry, but alas Margaret, you and I never loved one another. You understand, not only did I not love you – you didn't love me either.

Following this, as always, was a short pause. And then Margaret said:

— I knew that. And I also feel precisely the same way. I didn't want to tell you about this at the end of our lives, I thought, what difference could it make now what happened before, now, at the end of our lives, we're both eighty-four years old, and I thought, what happened before has passed and will never come back – but it seems it's come back. You brought it back, Albert. And so, I'll tell you what I never would have told you if you hadn't started this yourself. True love can only be mutual love, this I know. All these years Denny and I were lovers. We met almost every week. And sometimes travelled together – remember my business trips when I was younger, you didn't even notice that they sometimes coincided with various departures of your friend Denny. There were times we wanted to confess everything to you and change our lives entirely. But we didn't know that Sandra loved you, and you yourself didn't know that you loved Sandra. After all we appreciated you both so much, and didn't want to destroy our friendship. And we didn't want to inflict pain just for the sake of our own happiness. We decided to sacrifice our love to the circumstances. We loved each other, we suffered, but all the same we were happy. When Denny died, I couldn't even come to see him, to say goodbye. I couldn't be there because I couldn't bear it if Sandra had found out. Denny and I had agreed ahead of time that when one of us died, the other wouldn't come.

And here, Margaret couldn't bear it any more and began to cry. Albert sat there silent, still. He was probably in a state of shock. He didn't say anything, and didn't even try to calm his wife. And there they sat, Margaret bawling, Albert looking off somewhere in front of him. Two old people, strangely living out their lives.

Finally, Margaret calmed down and said:

— If you had realised earlier, Albert, that you love Sandra, and if you had told me about it, maybe we could've changed our lives and been happy. But that didn't happen. I guess that's how it was meant to be. Love can only be mutual, I agree with you, Albert, and forgive me for this cruel sincerity.

Pause.

Second Man I want to tell you about Denny.

First Man Yes! Sorry to interrupt, I just wanted to say – this is a really important detail – I wanted to say that Sandra and Denny were brother and sister. We forgot to tell you about that. They were brother and sister, only from different mothers. They were brother and sister by the same father, Denny was the child of their father's first marriage, he grew up with his mother, and he and Sandra met when Denny was thirty and Sandra was twenty-seven. And right away they fell in love with each other and got married. Naturally, their entire family was against the marriage, especially their father. But they didn't listen to anybody, they got married and cut off all relations with everyone, even with their father. Their father denounced them and never once went to see them till the day he died. So, yeah. That's all I wanted to say, sorry for interrupting. Continue.

Pause. The Second Man waits for something.

Yes and that too was a joke, they weren't brother and sister. Denny and Sandra were not brother and sister. That was a joke.

Second Man Yeah. So then. Now I'm going to tell you a story about Denny. The thing is that Denny was the kind of man who never, ever lied. One night, when Denny was eight years old, he couldn't fall asleep, and suddenly he saw a strange light through the window. Little Denny walked up to the window and saw a huge silver disc hanging in the sky. He saw a giant alien ship. A huge flying saucer. It shone with this blindingly magnificent silver light, the most radiant and beautiful light in the universe. The silver light was so wonderful, it was as though it gave off a kind of fragrance. The disc wasn't made of metal or of any other familiar material. It was like a flattened crescent moon. It was as if a crescent moon were straightened out into a flat disc. The whole disc consisted of this silver, or rather, lunar light. It was so beautiful, this moonlight, it was as though the whole universe had wanted for Denny to feel a soft, pleasant, even sweet chill go tingling along his spine. And here, a pleasant and sweet chill indeed went tingling along Denny's spine. And this eight-year-old boy stood before the window and looked spellbound at the resplendent spaceship. Denny was simply stunned by this magical light, this most beautiful, most wonderful light in the whole universe. He stood and stared at the miraculous sight. And then he thought perhaps he should run and wake up his parents. But for some reason he suddenly froze, scared. He was scared that when he went to wake up his parents, the spaceship could disappear and then his parents would of course never believe him, and then all this beauty that he'd seen would in one second be turned into the fantasies of a little boy. And here Denny realised that no matter who he told about what he had seen, nobody would ever believe him. Nobody. And that what he saw right now, the whole of this truest of miracles, this greatest, most wondrous light in the universe, would be turned into plain old make-believe. And then Denny suddenly understood the nightmare unfolding here on Earth. He understood that because people often lie to each other – and precisely for this reason – because people constantly tell one another lies, no one believes anyone any more. Nobody. And this simple thought came into his mind. And Denny, gazing into this light, the most beautiful light in the universe, gazing at the flying saucer hanging in the sky, quietly swore he would never, ever lie to anyone. Never, never, never, no matter what happened. And Denny kept his oath. To his death he never told a lie. Of course, sometimes, if nobody asked, he could choose not to tell, as for example was the case with the flying saucer, which he never revealed to anyone. And only one person in the world knew this story. That person was Sandra. Because Denny loved her very much.

First Man Now I'll tell you a story about Denny and Margaret. Denny and Margaret met each other a year before Denny met Sandra, because Margaret became the wife of Denny's best friend Albert. And when Denny and Margaret met each other, they immediately struck up a very intimate friendly relationship. Albert was surprised how quickly his wife got along with his friend. They became perfect pals. A year later, Denny met Sandra. He brought a photograph of Sandra to Margaret, and asked her what she thought of his new girlfriend. To which Margaret replied that she liked the girl very much, that Denny had good taste. And then, when Denny decided to propose to Sandra, he again came to Margaret and asked her, what did she think about the fact that Denny wanted to marry Sandra? And Margaret answered that it was a great idea, that she congratulated Denny and wished him and his future wife happiness.

Denny and Margaret were the most perfect of friends.

Pause.

Albert was quite taken by the friendship between his wife and Denny.

— Sometimes I don't understand, Denny, said Albert, who are you better friends with, me or Margaret?

— Are you jealous? asked Denny.

— Very. I want to be the only one in your life, joked Albert.

— Sorry, but I've got Sandra too, so that makes at least three of you, joked Denny.

One day, when Denny and Margaret were about forty years old, they sat on the patio at Denny and Sandra's house. They were alone. Sandra and Albert were somewhere in the garden. Denny and Margaret sat across from each other at the table. Denny rocked his leg back and forth under the table. And suddenly, his leg brushed against Margaret's leg. Denny and Margaret brushed against one another's legs under the table. And then Margaret unexpectedly said:

— Tell me, Denny, what do you think: could you and I sleep together? Or let me put it differently, what do you think: could you and I be lovers? Only please, answer me seriously, because I'm not joking.

Denny looked at Margaret very, very strangely. Very, very strangely. He put his hand on hers and he said:

— No, Margaret, we can't be lovers, because I love my wife very much, and value my friendship with your husband.

As for what Margaret said to her husband Albert about how she and Denny were lovers – she was just joking. After all we know that Margaret was a woman with a very fine sense of humour.

First Woman Now I'd like to tell you about this one evening. One evening, Denny and Sandra sat in the living room of their home with the lights turned off, they sat in complete darkness and looked through the window at the stars. It was winter, the children had left town to be with Denny's mother for Christmas holidays. Denny and Sandra were alone. They sat and looked at the stars. It was a clear, starry night. And suddenly Denny felt something. Something extraordinary, something exalted and divine. He suddenly felt very, very good, sitting there close to his wife, looking at the stars. And so he all of a sudden decided to tell Sandra about the episode from his childhood when he saw an alien spaceship. And Denny told Sandra the story of how he saw a glowing spaceship and about the silvery light radiated by the ship and even about how he decided he would never lie again to anyone.

Pause.

And then at the end of his story, Denny kind of bashfully asked Sandra:

— Well, you believe me – right?

Pause.

And there, at that very moment, Sandra realised that life is composed of these tiny, multicoloured fragments. That life holds nothing whole, just these paltry, tattered pieces, that there's no single plot, just a multitude of episodes, that there's nothing central, just trivialities and details. And that all these details can't seem to converge into something complete, into something consummate. It's probably impossible to explain all this with words, but Sandra suddenly felt that the world she lived in was missing something complete, something unified, some one thing that could connect all of this. She looked at Denny and she thought, 'My goodness . . . this is absolutely no place for aliens.'

Pause.

Second Man And now I want to tell you about Albert. Albert was a very good man. And now you'll find out why. One night Albert woke up because outside, someone was throwing pebbles at his window. Margaret was sleeping soundly and didn't hear anything. Albert got up, went to the window – no, there was no flying saucer and the pebbles were not being thrown by aliens. Albert looked out the window and saw his friend Denny outside. Denny gestured for Albert to come down. Albert got dressed and went outside. This conversation took place in August 1974. Denny and Albert were then about thirty-five years old.

— What's happened, Denny? asked Albert, bewildered.

— Albert, I have to tell you something very important. It concerns all of us. I can't sleep. I have to tell you everything I've got on my mind. Hear me out.

Albert said:

— Well, of course, Denny, let's go on to the patio. We can put on the kettle and have some tea or coffee. And they went on to the patio and there on that patio Denny delivered his ardent soliloquy.

He said:

— Albert, you and I are friends. You're the closest friend I have. There's no one in my life closer to me than you, except Sandra. I want to confess something to you. But please, hear me out to the end and don't interrupt. It's very important that you don't interrupt and that you hear me out, I won't speak long. Now listen. You know that I love my wife Sandra very much. And it's true, it's absolutely so. I love her more than anyone in the world, and to be honest, I love her much more than my children. Sandra is not only my wife, she is also my friend. And I love her not only as the mother of my children, not only as my friend, but also as a beautiful woman. You wouldn't disagree with the fact that Sandra is quite beautiful, would you?

Albert wanted to give his affirmation, but Denny wouldn't let him get a word in. He went on.

— Sandra is a very beautiful woman. And all these years I've admired her. I've never been satiated by her beauty, I've never gotten used to her beauty. Every day I look at her and I fall in love with her again and again like a little boy. I love Sandra, I'm happy living with her. We're very happy in bed together. I am content, content with everything. Sandra is my ideal. I want to live with her to my death. I never cheated on her and I don't plan on doing so. My dream is to live with her into old age and as I lie dying, to take her by the hand and tell her the most important, truthful, most touching words that I can find in my heart.

— Why do you think you'll die first? Albert managed to fit in.

— I don't think that, it's just what I dream of. I dream

26

not of dying first but of having the chance at the end of my life to tell Sandra the most important words I have for her. But that's not the main thing. Albert, once again I want to repeat that I love Sandra with the truest, most genuine, most beautiful love on earth . . . but . . . I nearly die from sexual desire every time I see your wife Margaret. I dream about sex with your wife almost every night. There's nothing I can do. It's against my will. When I see Margaret everything inside me turns upside down. My head starts spinning, my teeth chatter. It was like that from the moment we first met, but then I decided I could handle it, and indeed shortly after that Sandra appeared in my life and for a time I stopped thinking about your wife. But not too long ago everything came back again, especially now, in the summer, when women walk around in those damn summer dresses. Albert, I don't know what this is. But it's not just appeal. You understand I go to bed thinking about Margaret, I dream about her at night, I wake up and I think of her and even, sorry, but even when I make love to Sandra, I try not to, but I think about Margaret. I'm absolutely going crazy. I can't listen to her voice, I can't be near her. I can't see her hands, I can't see what a wonderful, kind, intelligent person she is. What an amazing sense of humour she has. When she's around, you see the whole world differently. My God, what a joy it is that this world is blessed with a woman like your wife Margaret. Thanks to her presence, I believe that the world is not without meaning, the world has meaning and that meaning is given to us by Margaret, by her smile, her way of being. One glance of hers fills this world with meaning and beauty. If the world has Margaret, the world has beauty, and if the world has beauty, there's a reason to live. All these thoughts have been coursing through my mind, my friend. And I admit I'm very, very tired of them. I don't know what all this is. Albert, tell me, what is this?

— It's love, man, replied Albert, calmly.

And Denny fell on the floor, curled up into a ball and cried like a baby.

— I love my wife Sandra, bleated Denny through tears. I know what love is, love can only be mutual love.

— You love Margaret, replied Albert just as calmly.

— No, I don't want to, I don't want to, it's not true, not true, Denny howled on.

And then when Denny had regained control of himself, sat down and sipped some hot tea, Albert once again, very, very calmly said:

— You love Margaret, Denny. What you've described, the feelings and sensations you've experienced, all of these are nothing other than the most sure-fire symptoms of love. You love Margaret, man, there's no doubt about it.

— But I'm telling you, I love and want to love Sandra. Here, for example, if right now I had to choose who I'd live with – sorry for saying so, Albert –

— It's all right, man, it's all right, replied Albert.

— But it's just an example, continued Denny. — If I had to choose right now whether to be with Sandra or with Margaret, I swear to you, without thinking even for a second, I would choose Sandra. I don't want to live with Margaret. I'm happy with everything living with Sandra. Everything, you understand, absolutely everything. And I don't think Margaret is prettier or sexier than Sandra. I am happy with everything. I love Sandra, and not Margaret. But why I can't even take a step without thinking only of your wife, I don't know.

— I know, said Albert, and you know too, man. Let's not deceive ourselves, after all, as far as I know I can't remember a single instance of you lying as long as I've known you.

— What, then, is love? very naively demanded Denny.

— It's precisely that same feeling you experience in the presence of my wife, responded Albert, wisely.

This scene was reminiscent of a dialogue between father and son. Denny resembled the young boy, who had come to his wise old dad to ask what love is. And Albert was just like the wise old dad, who knows that a time comes when love knocks on a young man's heart, and now was the moment when, according to the old family tradition, the father must tell his son of the elements of love.

— But then how do you define the feeling I feel for my wife Sandra?

— It looks to me like you just get along well together, Denny, that's all.

Here, Margaret appeared on the veranda. She had been awakened by Denny's heart-wrenching sobs, but of course Margaret didn't hear what he had been saying. Which is precisely why she came out on to the patio, to find out what two men could possibly be up to at two thirty in the morning.

— Good evening, said Margaret, sorry to barge into your conversation but . . .

At that moment, Denny's face turned white as a porcelain plate. Denny rose from his chair, fumbled at the air with his hands, staggered and fell on the floor. He had lost consciousness.

Albert was a very good man. He of course never said a word to Margaret about his conversation with Denny. Which of course meant he had to lie to Margaret, he had to tell her that Denny had had a severe nervous breakdown, connected with the fact he had just turned thirty-five, and that Denny was at the beginning of a mid-life crisis – and that such crises are particularly painful for men. Albert lied to Margaret, because he wasn't the sort of man like Denny, who never lied – Albert was an ordinary, very good man.

Pause.

Immediately following this event Denny and Sandra left on vacation for three months. They went to Australia, because Denny had wanted very much to visit another continent. And when they returned in three months, Albert and Denny went on being friends as though nothing had ever happened. Everything returned to its rightful place. And both of these beautiful couples went on living and ageing together.

First Man Here's a very funny story about how one day Albert got high on cannabis. One day, when Albert was already forty-eight years old, he decided to try smoking marijuana. It so happened that a student of his offered him a joint. I'm not going to get into all the details here, I'm not going to talk about what kind of 'weed' this was, where the student got it from or why he decided to offer marijuana to his professor . . . Actually, I think I will go ahead and tell you about that. This student offered marijuana to his professor because at a lecture Albert was giving, the theme turned to the use of hemp in the manufacture of nautical rope – it turns out a very large quantity of nautical rope is made precisely of hemp. And here, talking about nautical rope, Albert let on that he had never in fact tried smoking marijuana. In short, a student of his jokingly offered to get his professor high. And Albert, much to the surprise of his student, agreed. And not only did he agree. He took the joint and smoked it.

Pause.

And when he had smoked the joint, in literally a few minutes' time, he could suddenly feel that the world, the world surrounding him . . . well, how can I say this . . .?

Basically, the world . . .

In short, it became soft.

Albert stretched out his hands in front of him and touched the world. The world was soft. Albert stood with his hands stretched out in front him and suddenly, he started sobbing.

— Do you need help, Mister Professor? asked the student, terrified.

— No, answered Albert through tears, I'm fine, it's just I realised something about the composition of the world.

— And what is it you've realised about the composition of the world? enquired the student, hardly able to keep from laughing. It was unbearably funny for him to see his professor high.

— It's soft, pronounced Albert in a strange voice. — I always thought it was solid, but it's very soft and that's just unbelievable and very, very sad. Sad because in our regular state of mind, we don't notice this, and we live in a solid world.

And Albert touched the world with his hands again and again, bewildered by its softness.

And all this went on for as long as the marijuana held its effect. And then when the drug's effect faded, and the world once again became solid, Albert wiped the tears from his eyes, thanked the student for the services rendered, and went home. And as Albert went homeward, the world around him solidified and solidified, such that when Albert reached the porch of his home, the world had become solid as a rock. Albert walked into his house, saw Margaret, and said:

— Honey, I am solid as an iron hammer.

As usual, Margaret had to try especially hard to smile at her husband's joke, although on the other hand, she had long since gotten used to the fact that Albert had a very peculiar sense of humour.

Second Woman And now I'll tell you a story about the disappearance of Margaret. One day Albert came home very late, at eleven thirty in the evening. He went into the house and after some time found that his wife wasn't there. He then called his friend Denny and asked if Margaret was over. But Denny answered that Margaret was not over, and that he and Sandra were already in bed. Albert then called a few friends and acquaintances who, it seemed to him, Margaret might have gone to visit, but she wasn't there. Then Albert called all his distant acquaintances, who Margaret doubtfully would've gone to see, but Albert called them anyway, just to make sure she wasn't there. And then he called Margaret's parents, who lived in another city, and startled them to death by asking them if by any chance Margaret was there. She was, of course, not there, but now Margaret's parents, too, had joined in on the telephonic search. The last thing Albert did was to dial up morgues and hospitals, and this took up a considerable amount of time. I just want to remind you that back then there were no mobile phones, and Albert was calling from a landline and had to wait each time for a connection. And then, when Albert had called the last hospital he knew of, where he was told that no Margaret of any kind had checked in that day, and Albert in exhaustion hung up the phone, at that very moment he heard Margaret's voice coming from the large wardrobe that stood in their room.

— I'm here, Albert, in the wardrobe, but you have to do something important to get me out of here.

Albert turned pale and almost lost consciousness. Pulling himself together, he threw himself at the wardrobe and tried to open it, but the wardrobe was locked.

— How did you get in there, Margaret? shouted Albert, panicking.

— I'm in the wardrobe, replied Margaret in a solemn, sacramental voice. Her tone frightened Albert because from that tone it seemed obvious that Margaret had lost her mind.

— You must retrieve me from here. From this world. And to do so you must sing. You must sing a magical incantation.

— How did you get in there, Margaret? cried Albert. Who locked you in there?!

— Denny locked me in. I asked him to do so. I want you to play with me, I'm asking you to play a game. Please, Albert, don't be angry, just play with me. It's a game, you have to think of this as a game. You have to get me out of this wardrobe, and to get me out of this wardrobe, you have to sing a magical song. Make up some magical song and sing it.

This of course was followed by a long argument. Albert yelled at Margaret, tried to break the wardrobe, but it was an old oak wardrobe, breaking it was simply impossible, furthermore Albert was beside himself and couldn't focus. Of course, in the end, Margaret got out of the wardrobe without any magical songs. She opened the latch from the inside and spread the doors open to either side. Albert looked at Margaret very carefully, trying to see if she had gone crazy or what the hell was going on here at one thirty in the morning?

And Margaret sat down on the floor and suddenly said:

— Don't be mad. I haven't gone crazy. I just wanted to play, you know? Sometimes in life a person has these moments, we'll call them 'moments of strangeness', when he just really wants to play.

— You mean that was a game? asked Albert, gazing at Margaret with 'a look of pain and anguish'.

— It's moments of strangeness, answered Margaret undismayed. And you know, I sat in that wardrobe for several hours, and never once had to pee – a curious thing, a woman's body, isn't it? joked Margaret, and smiled, looking at Albert.

Or, at any rate, tried to smile.

Second Man I'd like to tell you the story about Denny and the round stone. When Denny and Sandra were in Australia, one day, as they were hiking, Denny saw a large round stone, lying next to the road. It was an ordinary round stone the size of a horse's head. Denny and Sandra continued along the path past the stone, but Denny suddenly stopped. He felt a sort of strong affinity for that stone. It seemed to him that between him and that stone there existed a kind of special connection. And Denny went back to the stone and sat down on it. He sat on the stone and closed his eyes. And there he sat, on this stone, with his eyes closed for some time, until he heard Sandra's voice.

— Are you OK, Denny? asked Sandra.

— Yes, answered Denny, his eyes still closed. I just have to sit on this stone for a little while, sorry Sandra, do you think you could wait for me a bit?

— Well of course, Denny, I'll wait for you. If for whatever reason you feel you need to sit here on this stone then I, of course, will be happy to wait for you as long as necessary.

And Sandra started walking around Denny in circles, and Denny went on sitting and sitting on the stone with his eyes closed.

About an hour after Denny had seated himself on the stone by the road, Sandra couldn't hold it any longer and said:

— Of course I understand, Denny, it's probably absolutely necessary for you to sit on this stone, I have no doubt that you've got a very compelling reason for doing so, but what about me? What should I do? I've been walking around you in circles for an hour now, what am I supposed to do?

— Search for your place in the world, answered Denny.

— Do what? repeated Sandra.

— Search for your place in the world, replied Denny once more. Everyone must have his own place in the world. The tree grows in its place, the flower buds in its place, a bird flies on its own trajectory. Each human being, too, must find his own place in the world.

— That's a very interesting theory, dear, said Sandra. And what about you, have you already found your place in the world?

— Yes, replied Denny, I did find it, to be honest I found it quite recently, just about half an hour ago. This is my place. I'm sitting on it. This is my place in the world.

Sandra looked at Denny. Denny closed his eyes again and lowered his head.

Then Sandra turned her back to him and headed the other way. In the direction they'd come from. She went back to the town where they were staying. It was called

North Darwin. Sandra went back to the hotel, lay down in bed, covered her face and cried. She couldn't find her place. She couldn't find a proper place to live in. She couldn't find a place to live.

First Woman I want to tell you the story about Sandra and the pink stripe. One day Denny and Sandra went to Australia. And there they walked about on dusty roads, sat on round stones and marvelled at the magnificent landscape. It happened that during one of their hikes Sandra caught sight of a long pink stripe on the horizon in the distance. This long pink stripe was like a young girl's ribbon, stretched along the tops of the hills.

— Look Denny, said Sandra, do you see that pink line on the horizon? Do you think that's the refracted rays of the setting sun, or the reflection of something pink from the surface of the hills?

There was a short pause. Denny looked carefully in the direction of the horizon. He gazed at the pink line with the look of an expert calculating the cost of a painting at an auction. After some time, Denny finally said:

— You know, Sandra, I don't think you ought to dramatise your life so much. Yes, life is sad, yes, at times it lacks meaning, lacks any kind of permanence whatsoever, but in the end you have me, and I have you. And that itself is a giant stroke of luck, that you and I have each other.

Sandra looked at Denny and smiled. And they walked on silently, both in their own thoughts. Sandra thought of the pink stripe on the horizon.

And then she said:

— You know, Denny, every person ought to have something they can look at in a moment of despair and calm themselves. And that pink line on the horizon might just be that sort of thing.

— A pink line on the horizon is hardly a thing, is it, Sandra? retorted Denny sceptically.

— Yes, it's a thing, answered Sandra.

And Sandra and Denny continued along the road towards the hills, and they reached the top of a hill and saw before them a great, level plain. The sun hung in the distance along the horizon, and from its centre pink rays spread out in all directions.

— There's the real source of the pink stripe you were asking about. It's the sunset, said Denny.

And Sandra burst into tears. And she sobbed for forty minutes, and Denny didn't know how to help her. He was despondent himself. His heart was wrenched to see Sandra in such pain, but he didn't know what he ought to do. Denny sat on the ground with his head in his hands and began staring straight ahead in the direction of the horizon. There the pink line of the sunset was drawn across the plain. Denny sat and looked at the pink line. And all of a sudden, he calmed down. He felt – fine. He looked back and saw that Sandra had also composed herself – she sat behind him, behind his back and she too gazed at the pink line on the horizon, and she, too, was just fine.

Pause.

First Woman Well, the time has now come to tell you how all this came to an end. By the phrase 'all this came to an end' I mean that absolutely everything ended.

So now I'll tell you how Sandra died. She died something like this. After Margaret explained to her husband Albert that she had been his best friend Denny's lover her whole life – and you remember that in fact this wasn't true, it was just a joke, because Margaret was a woman with . . . Right, so. The news that Denny and Margaret allegedly

37

loved each other had a very bizarre effect on Albert. He felt absolutely no remorse at the fact that the woman he had lived with for fifty-two years apparently had cheated on him his whole life. To the contrary, he quite rejoiced at Margaret's announcement because now he was absolutely, irreversibly convinced that love could only be mutual love, requited love. And then he decided to go to Sandra's and tell her before her death that she was mistaken to think that love could be unrequited love, that he, Albert, had always loved her and that meant that their love was mutual. And that true love could only be mutual love. He wanted Sandra to die with these thoughts, because it was very important. And he took off to see her and found her still alive, and told her that he loved her and had always loved her and as an additional example he even told her about Denny and Margaret, so that before she died Sandra found out that Denny had been unfaithful to her his whole life and that apparently all the touching words he had said before his death were just lies. And that Denny apparently wasn't the sort of person who never lies, and that his story about aliens was also nothing more than fiction. And with these thoughts, Sandra died.

Second Woman And now I'll tell you how Margaret died. We all recall that Albert managed to visit Sandra before her death and tell her many interesting things. And Albert took leave of Sandra with the feeling of someone who's paid his dues, and he headed home. Approaching his house, he decided he'd sit for a little while on the patio. And he walked on to the patio, and sat there for some time in the wicker armchair. And sitting there in the wicker armchair on the patio, he remembered how almost fifty years ago right here on this very patio, Denny told him of his love for Margaret. And Albert pondered how, as it turned out, Denny had deceived him, it turned out that Denny was his wife's lover. Albert of course still didn't know that Margaret was joking, he thought Denny and Margaret had had an affair. But in spite of this Albert wasn't angry with Denny. He loved and respected Denny very deeply. He even considered how hard it must have been for Denny and Margaret to hide their love, he imagined how much they must have suffered because of all this. Albert was a very, very good man. He sat in the wicker armchair on the patio and remembered those words Denny had uttered here fifty years ago. He remembered how Denny spoke of Margaret. And he remembered Margaret. And he remembered what a beautiful woman she was. And he remembered her youth, remembered her gestures, her gait. Her lips. Her breath. He remembered her body, her figure, remembered all her lines and curves. He remembered her tenderness. Her intelligence. Margaret was a very kind, intelligent, subtle person. When she walked into the room, it was as though everything and everyone were blessed by her beauty. Margaret was a very simple person. She did not dilly-dally, she spoke quite plainly and looked in the eyes of the person she was speaking to. True, she could be sharp-tongued and sometimes liked to play jokes on people, but all this could be forgiven because within Margaret was love for others. And Albert thought, all in all he was lucky to have a wife like that, and in the end it was a wonderful thing they were together, and how delightful it would be now to come home, embrace Margaret, press his cheek to hers . . . And suddenly Albert jumped up – a new thought dawned on him. He suddenly thought, 'My God – what have I done – I love her!' And here Albert realised that all of today's love for Sandra, all of this was just a late-arrived flood of romance sprung from the heart of an ageing fool, that he had lived fifty-four years with Margaret, had been happy with her, that this indeed was love, that he had always loved and still loved Margaret. The mother of his children. A wonderful human being. An extraordinary woman. This was love! What else?

— I love her, cried Albert.

He suddenly saw that Sandra's words had just aroused a slumbering romantic sensitivity within him, Sandra's words had awakened his youth. It was just youth that had suddenly cried out within the heart of an octogenarian. Of course, he had never loved Sandra, even when he had so admired her for crying over the fried snail. He had never loved Sandra, only admired her at times, but he had always loved only Margaret. And this was the absolute truth!

— What am I doing? Silly old fart! yelled Albert, I love you, Margaret.

And he ran into the house as fast as he could to find Margaret and fall before her on his knees and confess everything. But here, for a moment, he stopped in his tracks. Another thought popped into his head and held him right there:

— So this means love can be unrequited love? After all, Margaret loved Denny –?

— But I love her, cried out Albert suddenly. But I love her, cried Albert. I love her, yelled Albert. To hell with concepts, I love you, Albert cried at the top of his lungs and ran up to the house.

— I love you, Margaret, Albert called out again from the threshold as he entered the house.

Short pause.

The door to the bedroom was closed. A piece of paper was fastened to the door with drawing pins, and on the paper was written: 'Dear, before you enter this room, you should know – I've hung myself there. Margaret.'

Albert opened the door to the room. Margaret hung there from a rope. She was already dead.

Pause.

First Man Now I'll tell you what happened next. Here's what happened. Albert called up the police and the paramedics. He didn't try to remove Margaret from the noose, thinking this would be better for the police, for the investigation into the cause of death. But really, to be honest, he was just afraid to touch Margaret. As for the cause of death, such causes are too profound for a detective or doctor to understand. The official cause of death, as announced shortly after, was suicide. On the table lay Margaret's suicide note. Albert took the note, went outside on to the patio, sat in the wicker chair, opened the note, and began reading:

'Dear Albert. I decided to do this because I have entirely ceased to understand how everything functions here. I don't understand how everything fits together, what follows what. I can't see the reasons why everything moves forward, develops. I can't find order, I can't find permanence. There's got to be some kind of permanence, right, Albert? There has got to be at least some kind of permanence in this enormous, shifting universe, Albert? There's got to be at least some kind of permanence in this shifting universe, Albert . . . ?'

And from here on, the whole page was inscribed with this single phrase. Apparently while Albert had been at Sandra's telling her about his love for her and about how Margaret and Denny had been lovers, all this time, Margaret sat at the table and wrote: 'There has got to be some kind of permanence in this shifting universe?' The whole page, on both sides, was inscribed with this one phrase. And at the end of the page were a few more lines. Here they are: 'Love can be unrequited love, because I, for my whole life, loved you, Albert. I love you. You're not to blame for my death. The only thing to blame for my death is this damned impermanence. I'm sorry. Goodbye.'

Pause.

Second Man And now we're left to find out how Albert died. After the deaths of Sandra and Margaret, Albert lived another ten years. He died when he was ninety-four years old. Here's how he died. Late one evening Albert sat on the patio in his wicker chair. It was already dark and Albert gazed up at the stars. From old age his vision was poor, and the great starry sky merged for him into a single flickering light-blue haze. And there Albert sat, looking at the flickering light-blue haze, and suddenly he remembered Margaret's last words, about how there's got to be some kind of permanence in this shifting universe? Albert uttered this phrase aloud, as though addressing his question to the universe itself, unfurled before him in its hazy, flickering light-blue form.

— There's got to be some kind of permanence in this shifting universe? Albert asked the universe.

And at that very second, his heart stopped.

That's how Albert died. And all this came to an end. Goodbye.

The Men and Women stand and leave the stage.

Curtain.